AF225724

Heimlich
Unheimlich

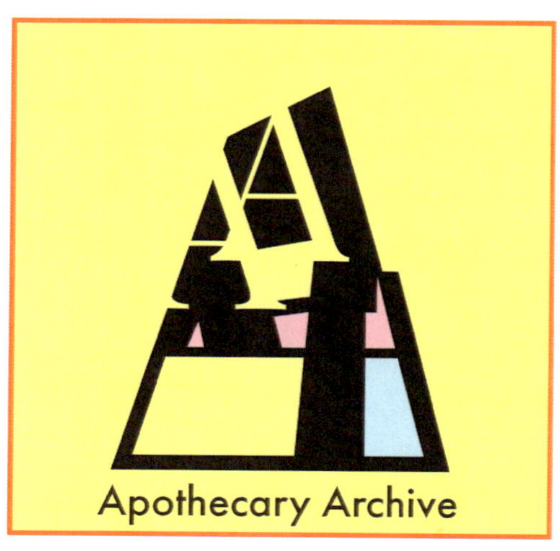

National Library of Australia
Catalogue-in-Publication entry
Authors: Hazel Smith and Sieglinde Karl-Spence
Title: Heimlich Unheimlich
ISBN: 978-0-6488079-9-5

Published by Apothecary Archive: 2024
https://apothecaryarchive.com/
Published on Gadigal land.

Book Design: Claire Grocott

Cover Image: Sieglinde Karl-Spence and Claire Grocott

Heimlich Unheimlich

a poetry and art collaboration

Hazel Smith (poet) and Sieglinde Karl-Spence (artist)

PREFACE

Heim in German means home, so *Heimlich Unheimlich* can translate loosely as *Homely Unhomely*. However, heimlich more usually means secretive or hidden, while unheimlich means uncanny, so the connotations of the two words can overlap. This relationship between heimlich and unheimlich (discussed in Sigmund Freud's essay 'The "Uncanny"') underlies this book.

Heimlich Unheimlich uses the contrasting childhoods of Sieglinde Karl-Spence and Hazel Smith as a starting point. It focuses on two characters who have names related to different kinds of cloth. One is Hessian, a German girl born towards the end of the Second World War, whose father fought in the German army. She migrates with her family to Australia when she is still a child and eventually becomes an artist.

The other is Muslin, who is born into a Jewish family in England after the war. She is a violinist who subsequently becomes a poet and migrates to Australia as an adult. Her family is preoccupied with preserving a Jewish ethnicity and avoiding antisemitism. Her relatives live in the shadow of the holocaust and are unforgiving of Nazi Germany. Both Hessian and Muslin are shaped by, but also rebel against, the cultural environments in which they grow up.

Heimlich Unheimlich suggests strong crossovers between Muslin and Hessian, intertwining and reconciling their different childhoods. It explores through texts and images the inter-generational after-effects of the Second World War (what Marianne Hirsch calls 'postmemory'), the blending of personal and historical trauma, belonging and migration.

It has considerable relevance to contemporary Australia and global issues concerning war, migration and ethnic identity.

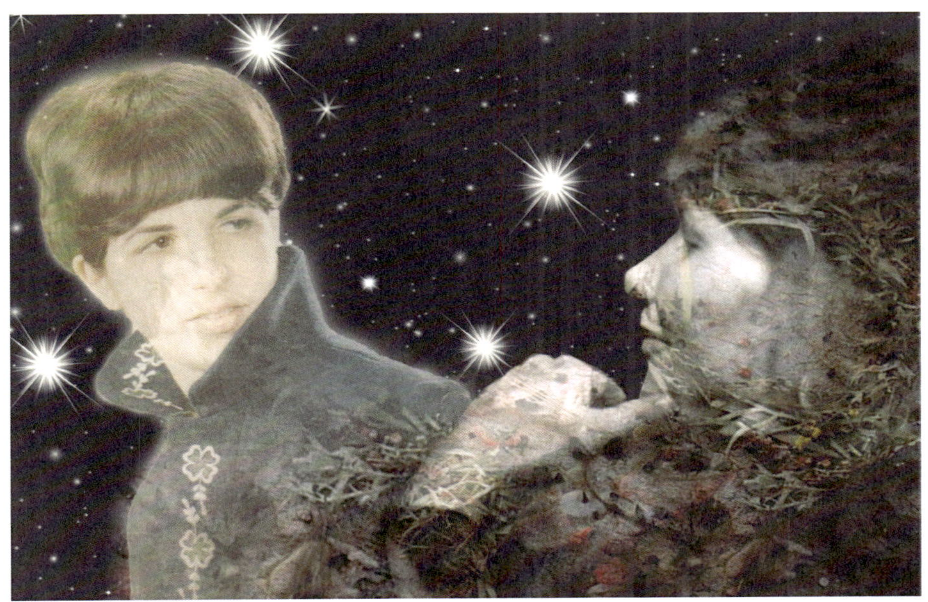

The book employs photographs from the family albums of Sieglinde Karl-Spence and Hazel Smith. Claire Grocott and Claire Letitia Reynolds were technical assistants and collaborators in the making of the visual images. The book design was by Claire Grocott.

The *Heimlich Unheimlich* project also takes the form of a gallery installation by Hazel Smith and Sieglinde Karl-Spence: this includes an art video created by Karl-Spence, Smith and Roger Dean and performed by the sound and multimedia group austraLYSIS. The installation has been exhibited in the Broadhurst Gallery, Hazelhurst Regional Gallery and Arts Centre, Sydney, 2020, the Edith Cowan University Gallery 25, Perth, 2021, and the John Mullins Memorial Art Gallery, Dogwood Crossing, Miles, Queensland, 2023.

The video was also selected for the Electronic Literature Organisation's Virtual Gallery Exhibition in 2020, *(Un)Continuity*, which was based in Orlando, Florida, USA.

ACKNOWLEDGEMENTS

We are migrant settlers who acknowledge First Nations people
as the original inhabitants of Australia.

We live and work on unceded Dharawal land and
pay our respects to elders past and present.

We would like to thank our publisher Gareth Jenkins for his interest in and
support of the book. We are also indebted to Claire Grocott for her fastidious
and inspiring work on the collages, Claire Letitia Reynolds for previous
important work on some of the collages and Roger Dean for his numerous
comments and suggestions. We would like to thank Myra Woolfson and
Inge Stocker for their assistance with translation.

Extracts from the book were published in *Axon*, volume 13, no 2.
https://www.axonjournal.com.au. Extracts were also shown on the
Osmosis Press site https://osmosispress.com/featuredwriting.

This book is dedicated to our friends and families.

CONTENTS

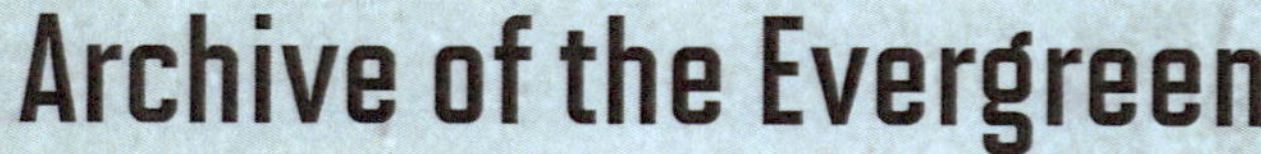

Archive of the Evergreen

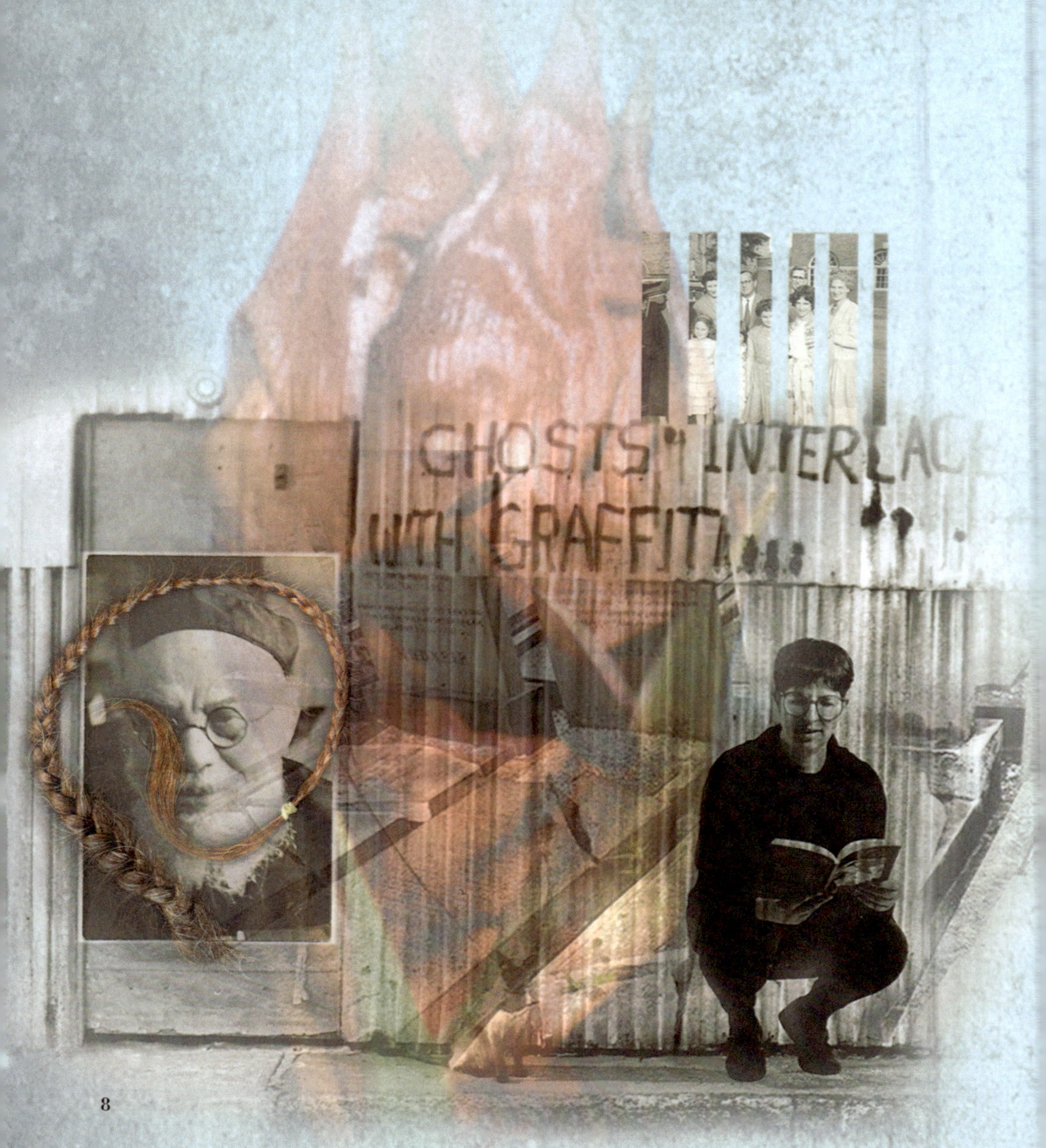

there are names in the computer-generated family tree
        Muslin has never even heard about
                places she does not know
                        Akmenė, Vilnius, Kretinga
                        they are just names to her

a family tree is a set of tags
        it does not disclose
                the lives of the people to whom the names belong
                        what they were like
                                the homes from which they were torn

                        there are dead shoots amongst the buds
                                messed up blossoms that have fallen off
                                        moist soil clinging to straggly roots

she scrutinises the tiny photographs of her great-grandparents
        they look like aliens but also welcoming

                        names repeat themselves
                                like automated phone calls
                                        through the generations

she remembers her mother
                sowing the seed of death in her
                        telling her how her great-grandmother lost her daughter
                                and afterwards did not smile for a year

                her grandfather's homestead ripped by fire in Lithuania

she wants to memorialise these people
        but also knows that a family passport
                does not necessarily mean a common cause

her grandfather wrote his memoir
        no one would publish it
                now it is on the internet
                        archiving an extinguished way of life

how euphoric he would have been to know
        his words were evergreen

Heimlich Unheimlich

heimlich unheimlich
heimlich unheimlich
heim   lich

         unheimlich un

                    words breed odd memes

bold illusionists
      misfits, activists

        words do not fit with
          the husks that house them

heimlich as home
the warm, the friendly, the intimate

heimlich as obscure
inaccessible to knowledge

        heimlich as the name for everything
        that ought to have remained
        hidden and secret

      'we call it unheimlich
      you call it heimlich'

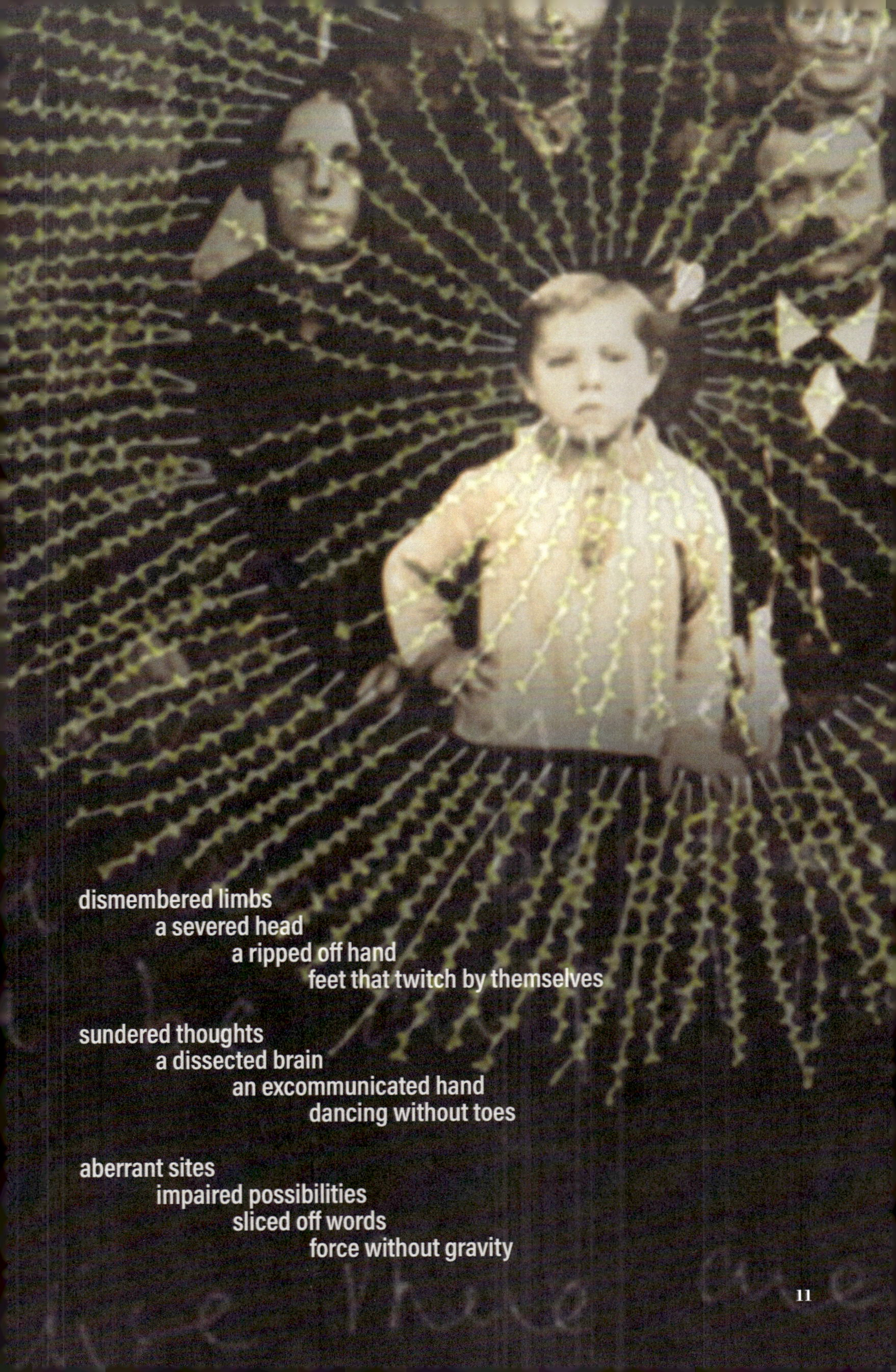

dismembered limbs
    a severed head
        a ripped off hand
            feet that twitch by themselves

sundered thoughts
    a dissected brain
        an excommunicated hand
            dancing without toes

aberrant sites
    impaired possibilities
        sliced off words
            force without gravity

From Rubble to Reliving

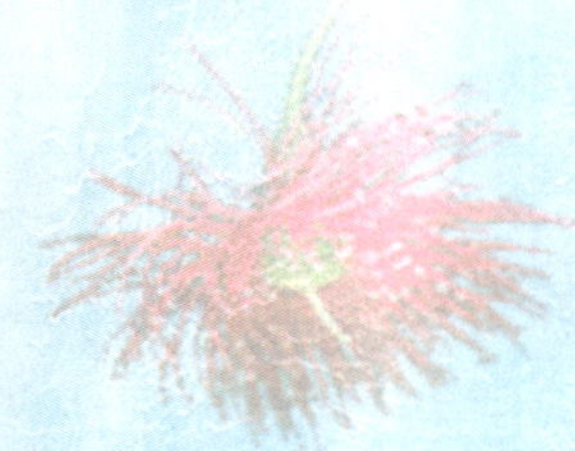

memory is
bricolage not reproduction
scraps scribblings
shreds slivers
mix reassemble

memory is a collage not a video recorder

slabs from several separate quarries
slip and slide
into a single building

such slabs predict
towering stone walls
less accurately
more readily

from rubble to reliving

the city fitted out with carpets of rubble
the splintered remains of cups and saucers
the arms and legs of psychotic buildings
severed from their familial torsos

windows punched through
victims of a boozy fight
roofs that have aerobically lifted themselves off
facades masking as theatrical props

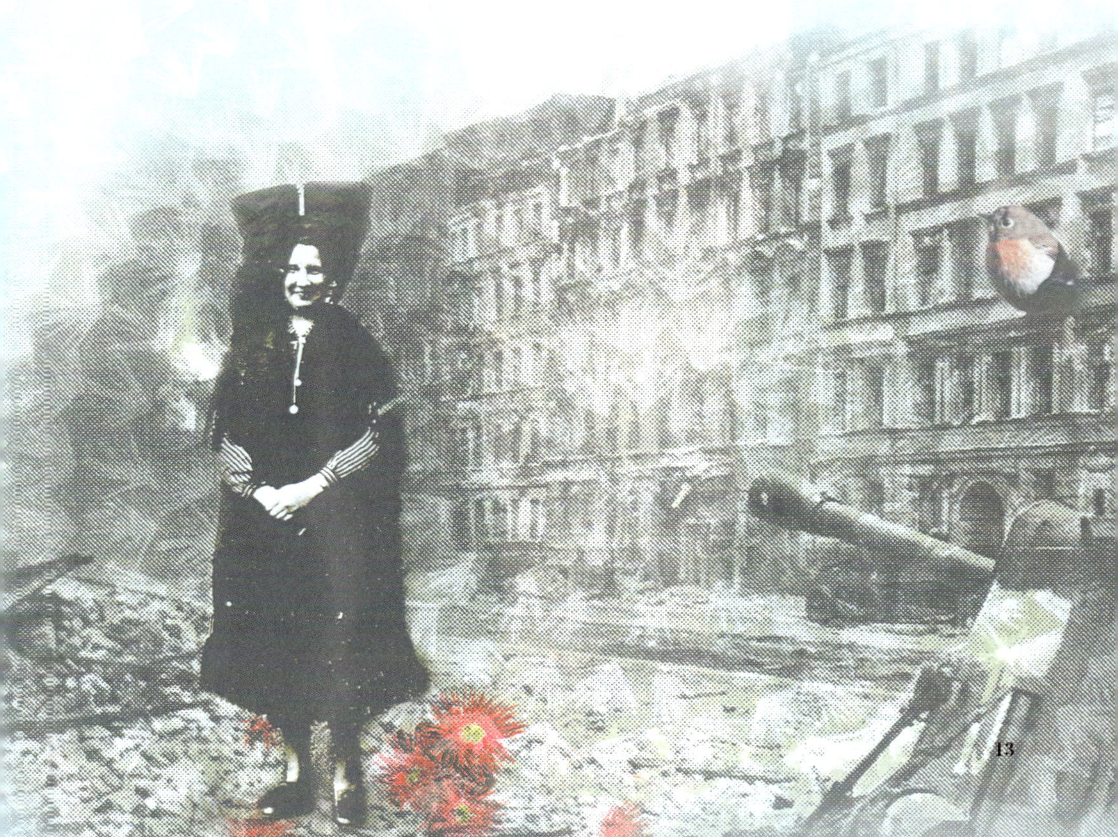

generation after generation
pounded and pummeled
the Nazi era
hoping for a
knockout blow
but the past always
picked itself up

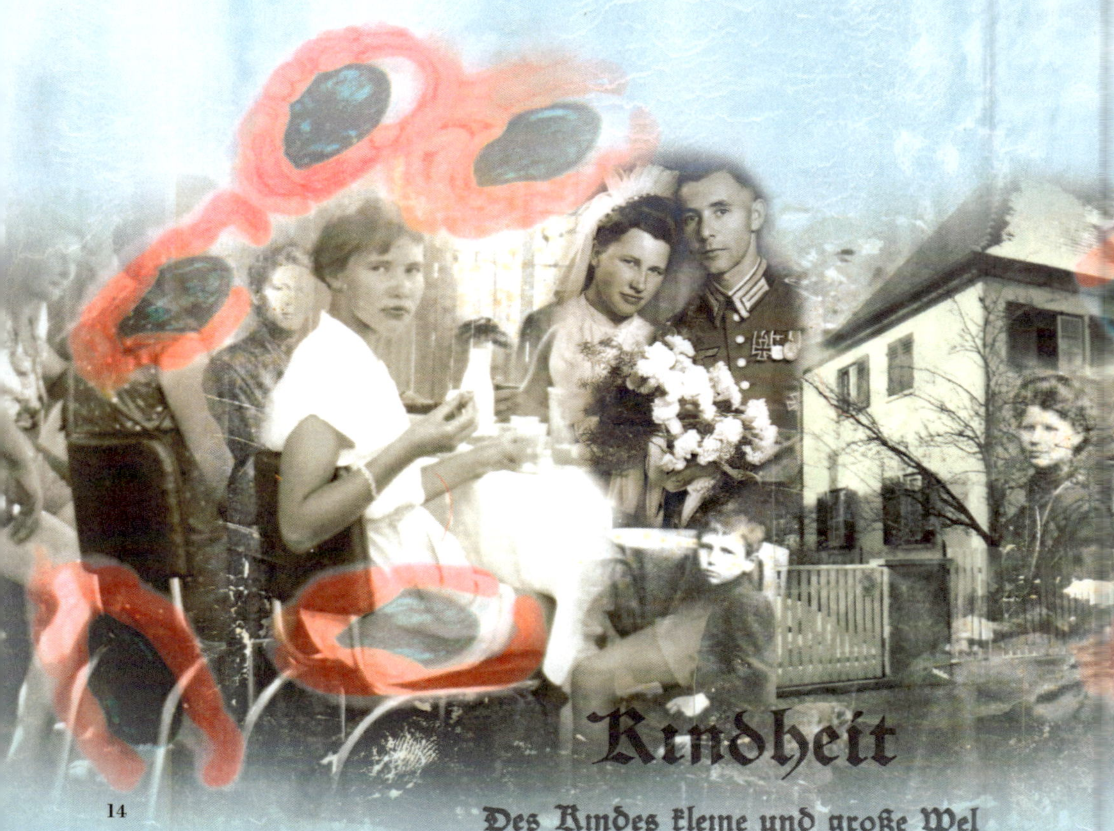

the Baader-Meinhof gang
children of a nauseous past
declared war on
fascist imperialism

they thought fighting it
would free them
but history is
a sly bully
and seriously
unforgiving

in 2015 a satirist
posted quotes
from Mein Kampf
and other Nazi literature
on the UK Daily Mail's website
substituting the word
'migrants' for 'Jews'

**hundreds of readers
'liked' the comments**

somewhere along the way they lost their histories
as if they were paper hankies falling
snowflake-like from their sleeves
they piece their trajectories together
from newspaper cuttings, faded photos

the woman walks around a small space
she feels safe in her tiny territory
pulls the walls inwards
hugging them to her
until they become a silk shawl
twirled closely round her

another woman is always trying
to climb out of the space
that bears down on her
she clambers again and again
only to fall back
but when she escapes
she runs and runs
past the borders of countless countries

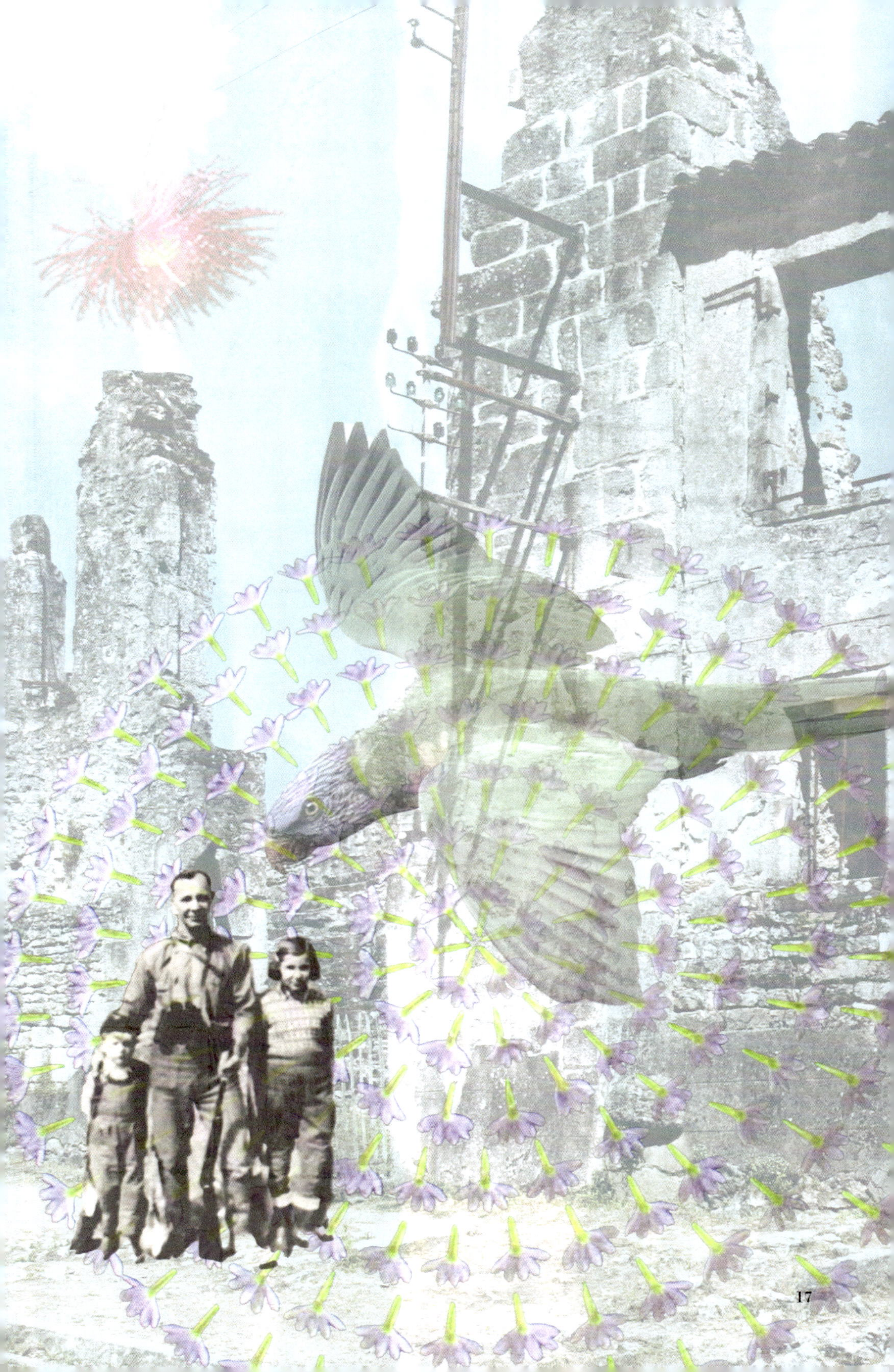

2 often use notebooks but
just for jottings. 2n a way
those jottings are interesting because
showing my process or at
least the beginnings of it. But
2 guess 2 was ambivalent
about using the Tapa
notebook in that way because
it is beautiful and because
the contents will be on public
display.

sometimes she scents
the language of her birth
the words do not matter
it is the sound
the texture
the hint of home

a home that can never be a home

when she hears German
strangers melt into intimates

sometimes she believes
it is her first language
though that is nonsense

she belongs in Australia
belongs in Germany
belongs in England

**belonging has always
been a faithless bedfellow**

The White Rose

She could not recall the moment of her conception, nor tell the story of her birth. But she did know that the day she arrived was marked by a giant-size absence, a large, non-fillable hole.

Her father, an officer in the German army, was fighting in Russia. The Germans had lost Leningrad and were retreating. That year German forces liquidate the Jewish ghetto in Kraków.

Later, when Hessian visualized her father, he was always walking backwards. Away, becoming more distant, his blurred face still holding her gaze.

Years later in Grafton: bamboo bending in the wind.

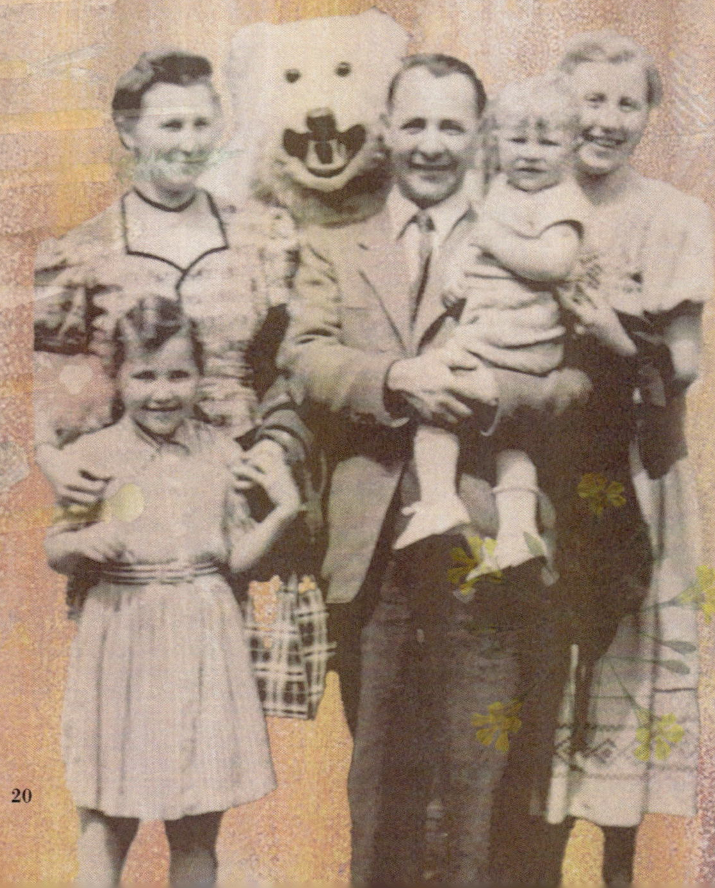

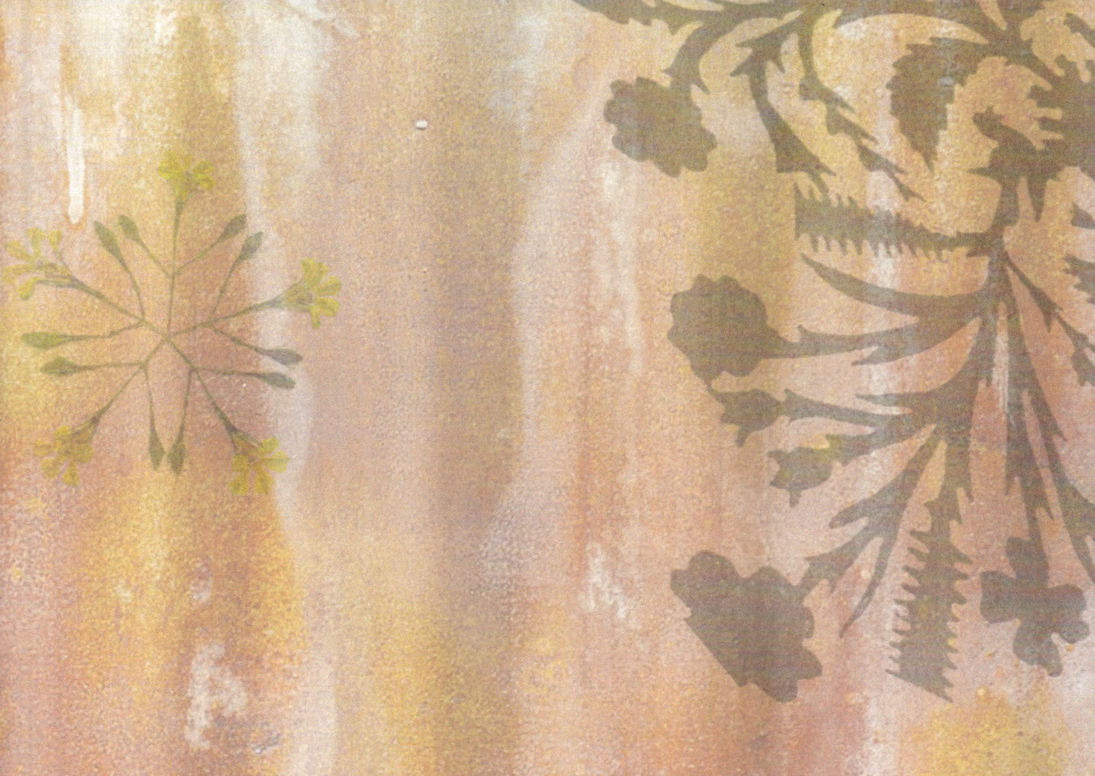

The White Rose. 1943. The year of her birth. Non-violent fighters, they were slaughtered.

Her mother is twenty when she gives birth to her
so frightened and homesick
she scratches on the wallpaper of her tiny room
on top of the Gaststätte.

Hessian is taken in a cradle to the air raid shelter under the house
'a raid on the inarticulate'
an assault on guilt and innocence
plundering simultaneity

She had to fill the hole to feel whole. But the hole was greedy,
insatiable. She threw waste into it. She tried stitching and
gluing. But a hole cannot be denied. It needs to breathe, make
remonstrations, gesticulate.

Sophie Scholl, aged 21, a member of The White Rose
showered her fellow citizens with subversive leaflets

Even after the fighting ended, her father seemed permanently angry.

Once upon a time there was a little German girl. She had a Tante Gisela who made her elegant dresses with matching hat and handbag. On the train to Germany she would sing a little song and passengers would put sweeties in her handbag.

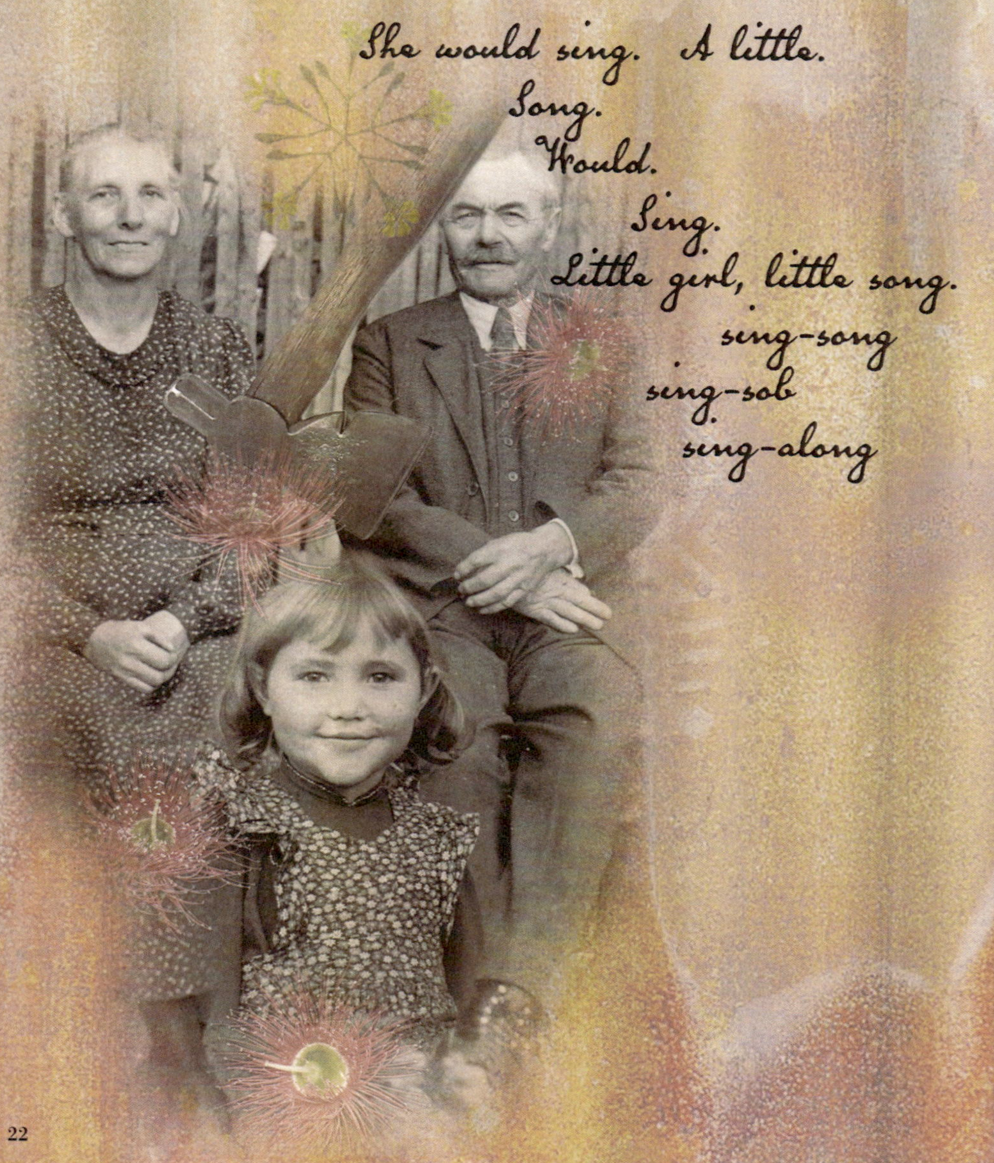

In her dream someone was running after her. She must not be caught. It was her grandfather. He was furious because — distracted by her antics with the bicycle wheel, which spun chaotically towards him — his axe slipped, cutting off his thumb.

After the war her father would venture out on the streets and pick up cigarette butts. He would pull them apart to make a pile of tobacco. The only means to make money.

Humpty Dumpty fell off the wall and tried to put himself back together again.

The water tanks. Sitting underneath them. Emerald-green moss thriving from the drips; the joy in making her own moss garden. The garden of Eden.
Later, recalling it, she mesmerised herself with mandalas.

Herman the German they called him
                    It is 1953 and Germans are not popular in Australia

                                        Her mother learnt impeccable English
        'That's not cricket' she would say, tone deaf to its upper-class English allegiances

There were always those whispering voices, augmenting into accusation
                            'You must have known
                                    Why didn't you do something?'

            She learnt the syntax of survival, firmly denied her German-ness.

Her parents' guilt:
        it was a tremulous foundation for everything that followed

                                    they found jobs on a farm
                                        fifteen miles from Griffith
        Her father a farmer, her mother a housekeeper

Dear Grandma, I miss you, wish I was a banana so I could be sent to you.
Missing seemed to be the main tonality of her life

She did not know if her parents loved her
maybe they did but did not know how to show it

They dressed her up for school in her German apron
The other children laughed and laughed and laughed

she would tear the apron off
when he found out she had discarded it
her father would beat her

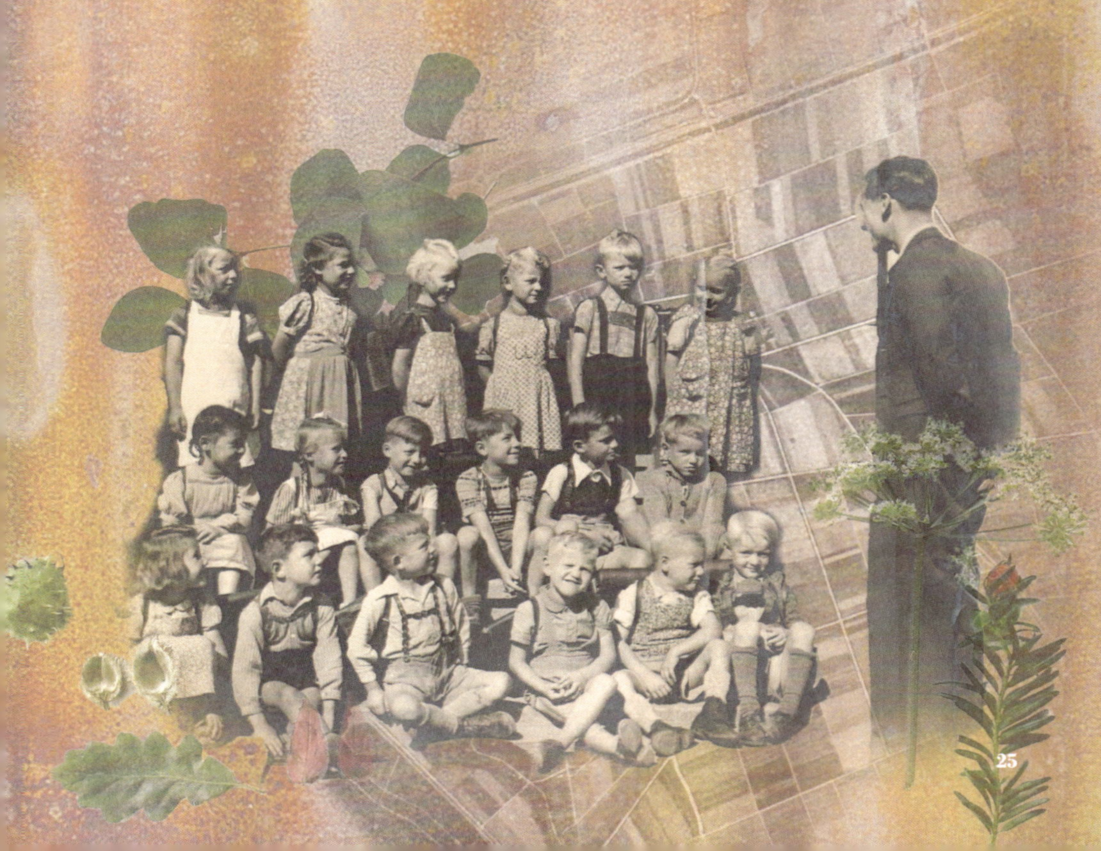

The Vengeful, Directive Angel

The branches of the family tree kept breeding uncontrollably. Language is permanently foetal; music is a high-wire act. She wanted to write her life truthfully with poetic falsification.

The girl in the dress with the lace collar is learning to play the violin. Smocking filled the mother's days, stretching nerves, cotton, tradition. Muslin was bored visiting elderly relatives, never thinking she'd be old one day. Ritual divorced from its sources divulged very little.

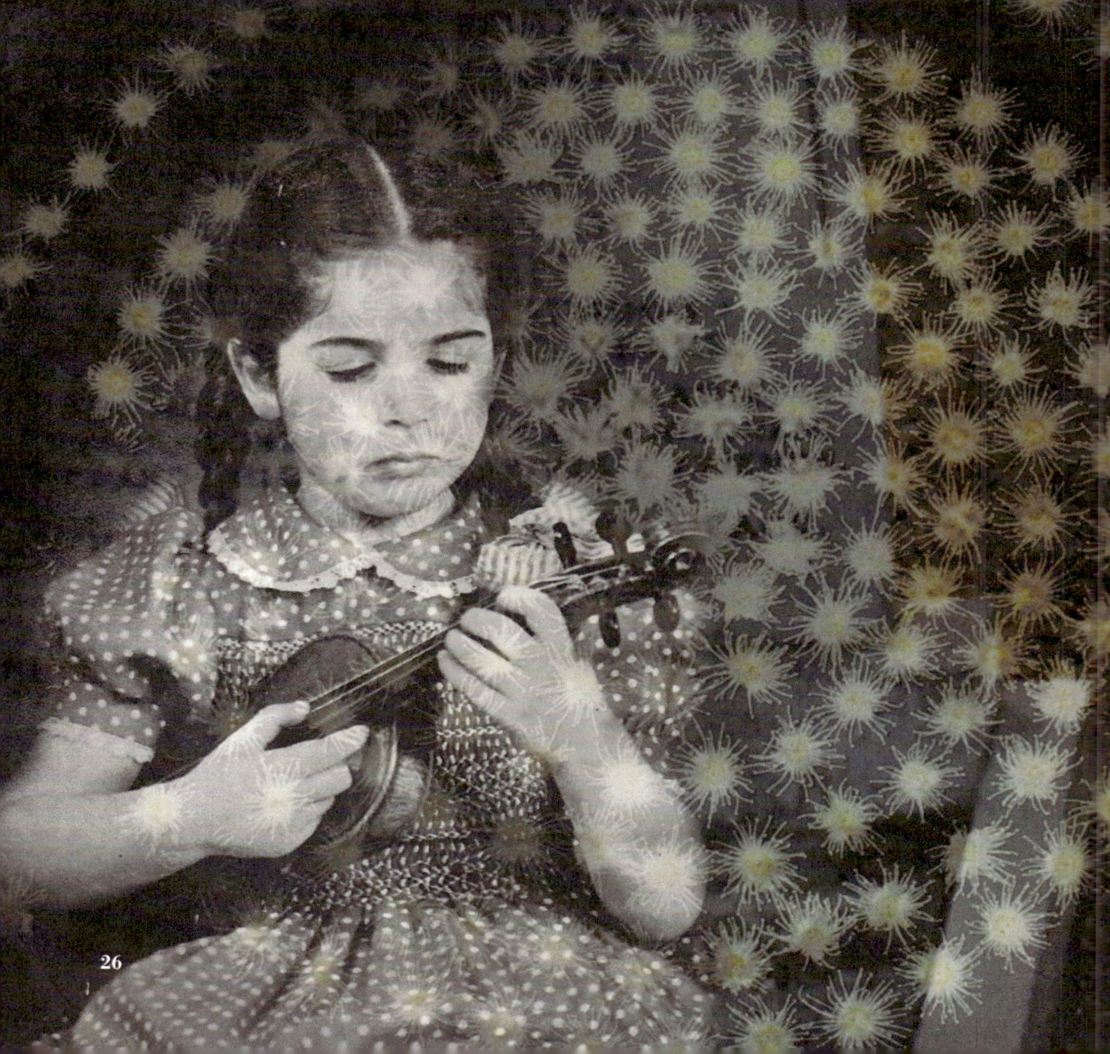

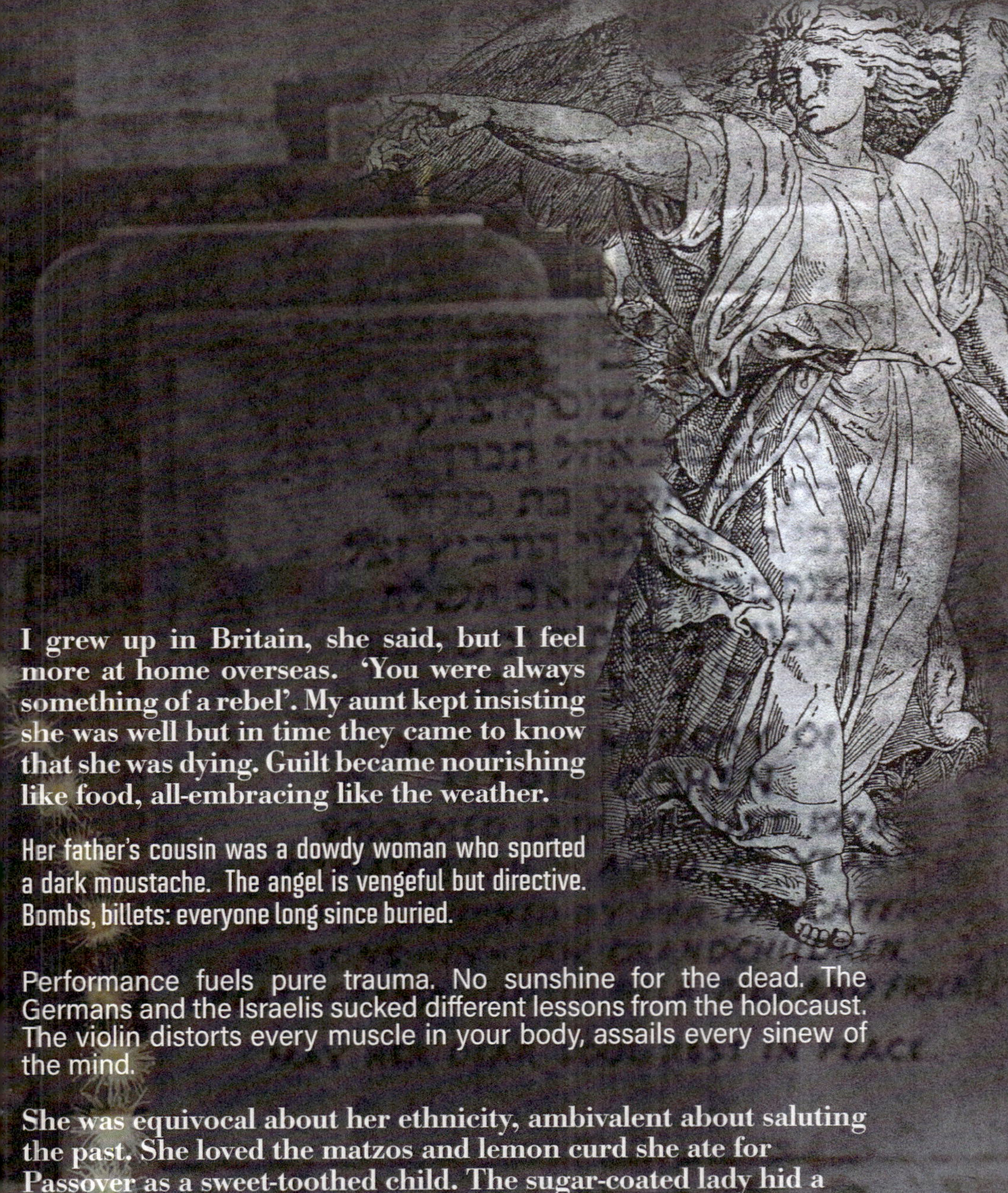

I grew up in Britain, she said, but I feel more at home overseas. 'You were always something of a rebel'. My aunt kept insisting she was well but in time they came to know that she was dying. Guilt became nourishing like food, all-embracing like the weather.

Her father's cousin was a dowdy woman who sported a dark moustache. The angel is vengeful but directive. Bombs, billets: everyone long since buried.

Performance fuels pure trauma. No sunshine for the dead. The Germans and the Israelis sucked different lessons from the holocaust. The violin distorts every muscle in your body, assails every sinew of the mind.

She was equivocal about her ethnicity, ambivalent about saluting the past. She loved the matzos and lemon curd she ate for Passover as a sweet-toothed child. The sugar-coated lady hid a Nazi past: she was deported once she was found out. 'Do I really have to leave forever', she said, 'or can I come back on a visit?'

Mill of Memory

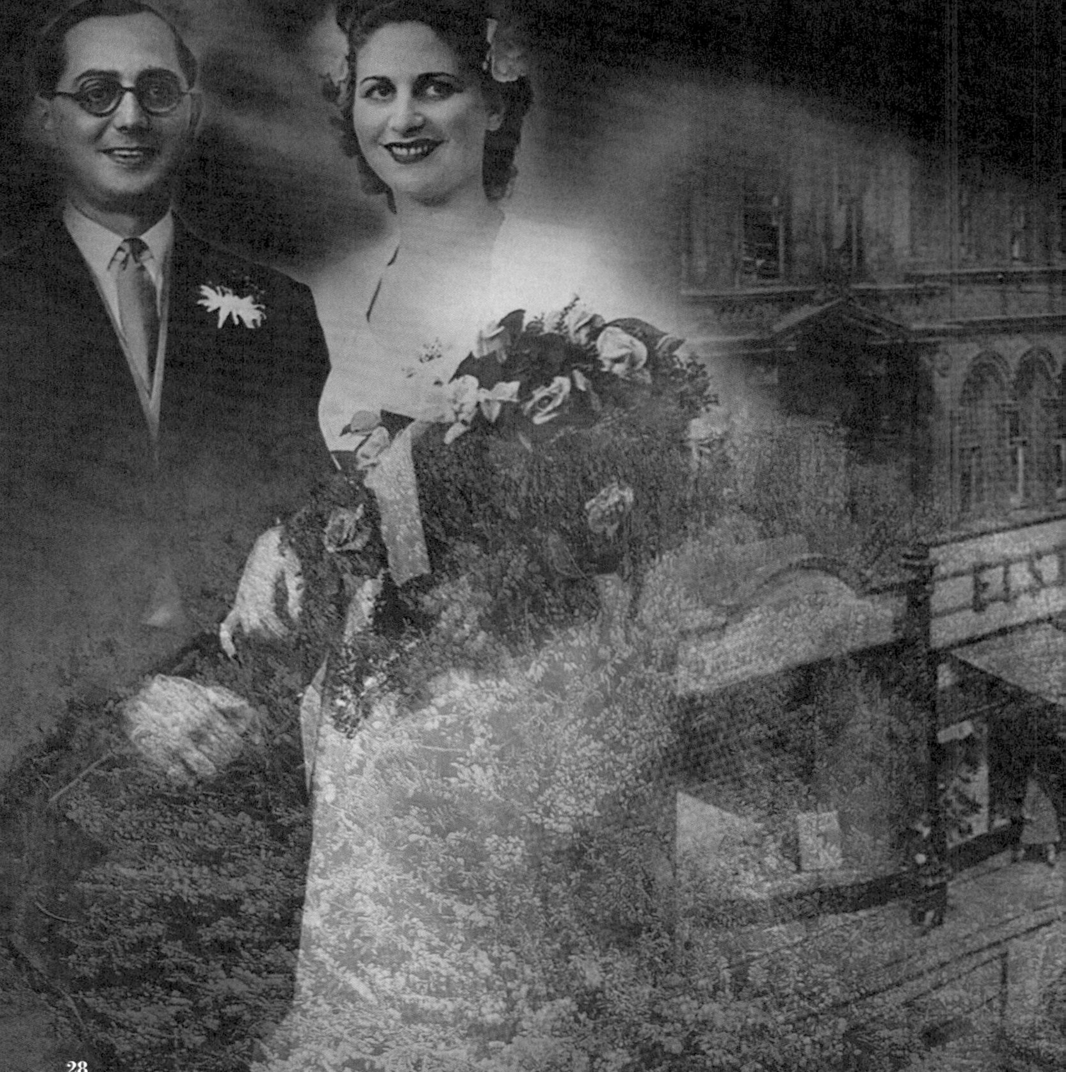

one moment time underachieving
                the next moment time running away with the prizes

Muslin clings to the clothes of the dead
        as if limbs not coverings

                on her key ring the redundant key still dangling

        when he died
                she had wondered who would sing Kaddish for him
            puzzled by this errant concern

so many unknowns she wanted to un-curtain

                        no one to ask

                            a generation
                        no longer bleeding

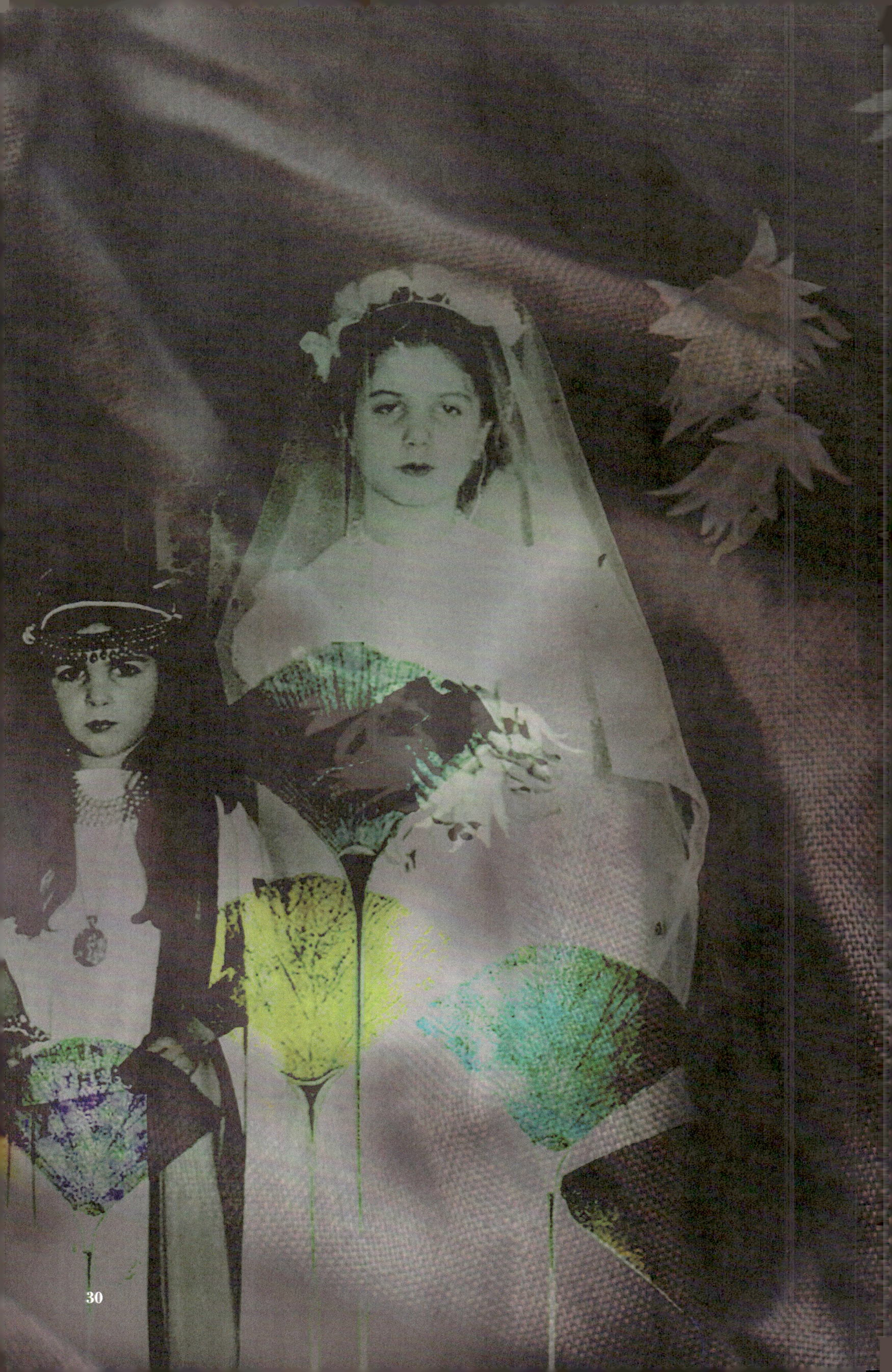

slightly bored
Muslin and her big sister watched *The Lone Ranger* every week
oblivious to the racism it rode

   boxed the television's ears
  to subdue the interference
  the screen black and white (and tiny)

     the shoot of excitement when
   her father brought home
    a medley of chocolate bars
     in a brown paper bag

       Saturday morning sleep-ins
        Sunday morning bagels
     never tasted so delicious again
      soft inside
        crispy on the outside

    the Norwegian au pair girl announced
       I will 'kunit' for the children

    the multi-coloured cardigans
     conjured with circular needles
      looped through the generations

    meanwhile the British empire was noisily dissolving
'the wind of change is blowing through this continent'

   Muslin learnt at school about kings and queens
    not about drudgery

    but when a relative from South Africa
     demeaned those with a darker skin
      she flexed her juvenile guns

her father used to vanish for long hours each day
        never risked a holiday

                the mill where he laboured
                seemed tumbledown to them
                not 'listed'

                        it was always known as 'the place'
                        like a child without a name
                        a faceless location

                        a rag-merchant
                he traded in recycled cloth
                        long before regeneration was in vogue
                (a thriving business until synthetics sundered it)

        the wool was shredded
        revivified by mixing, grinding

                                fabric's alchemy

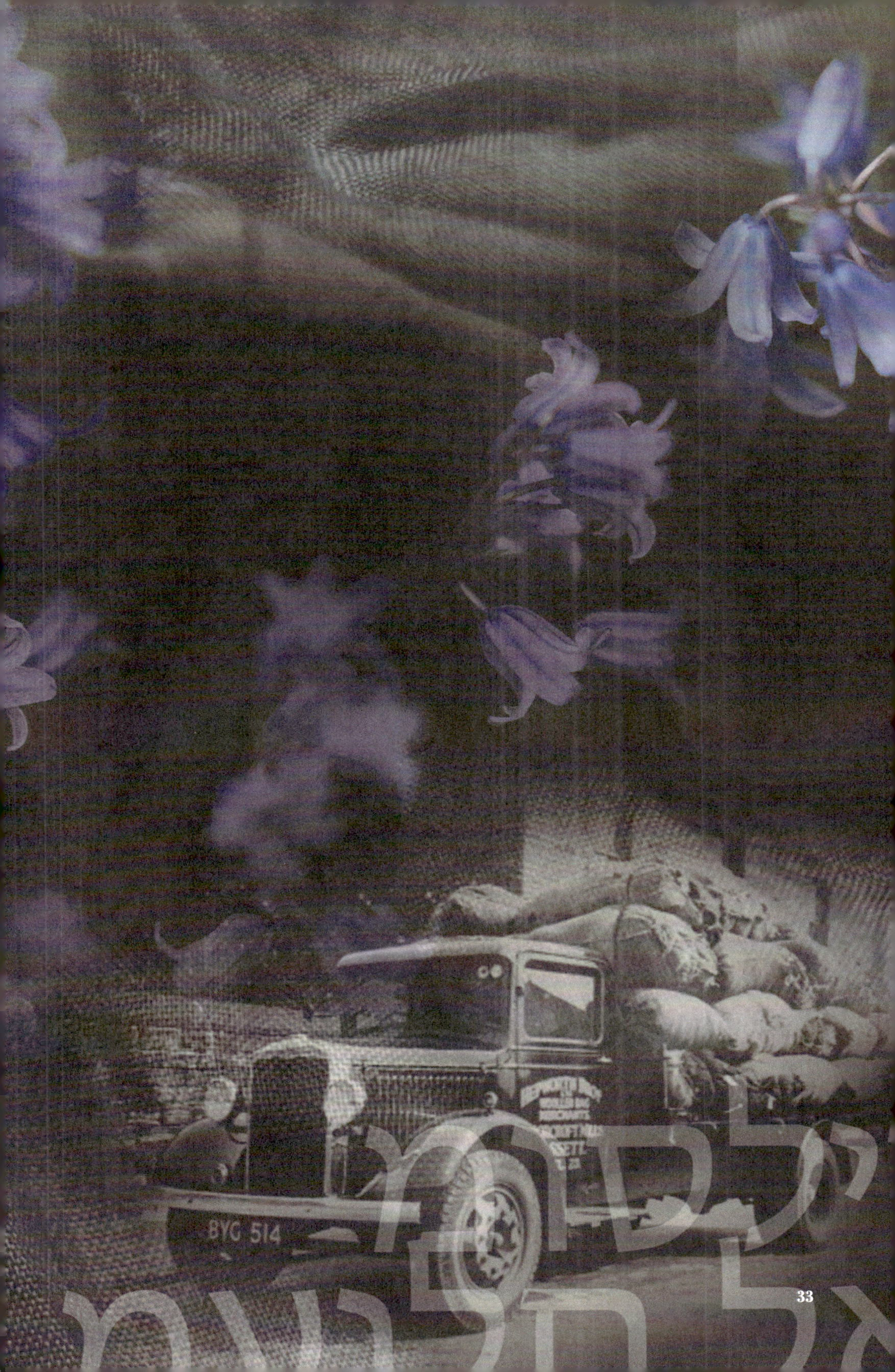
BYG 514

Muslin forensically inspects old pictures of the city
almost expecting to spot herself in them

she wants to summon the past
and vanquish it
both at the same time

Queen's Arcade 1889
Thornton's Arcade 1877-78
Grand Arcade 1897
The Corn Exchange 1863

(fast food now not corn)

The Town Hall black as soot until they cleansed it
Briggate in the 1600s, the crown prince of cloth markets

in the 1950s a bored Muslin
shopped in Schofields on the Headrow
with her weary, flat-footed mother

who regarded Leeds as unheralded adversary
too cold, too urban

Muslin never questioned
her mother's icy kinship with Leeds
did not cogitate whether the city was a scapegoat

treated her birthplace
with inherited disdain
only discovering its warm grace
when she was about to finally abandon it

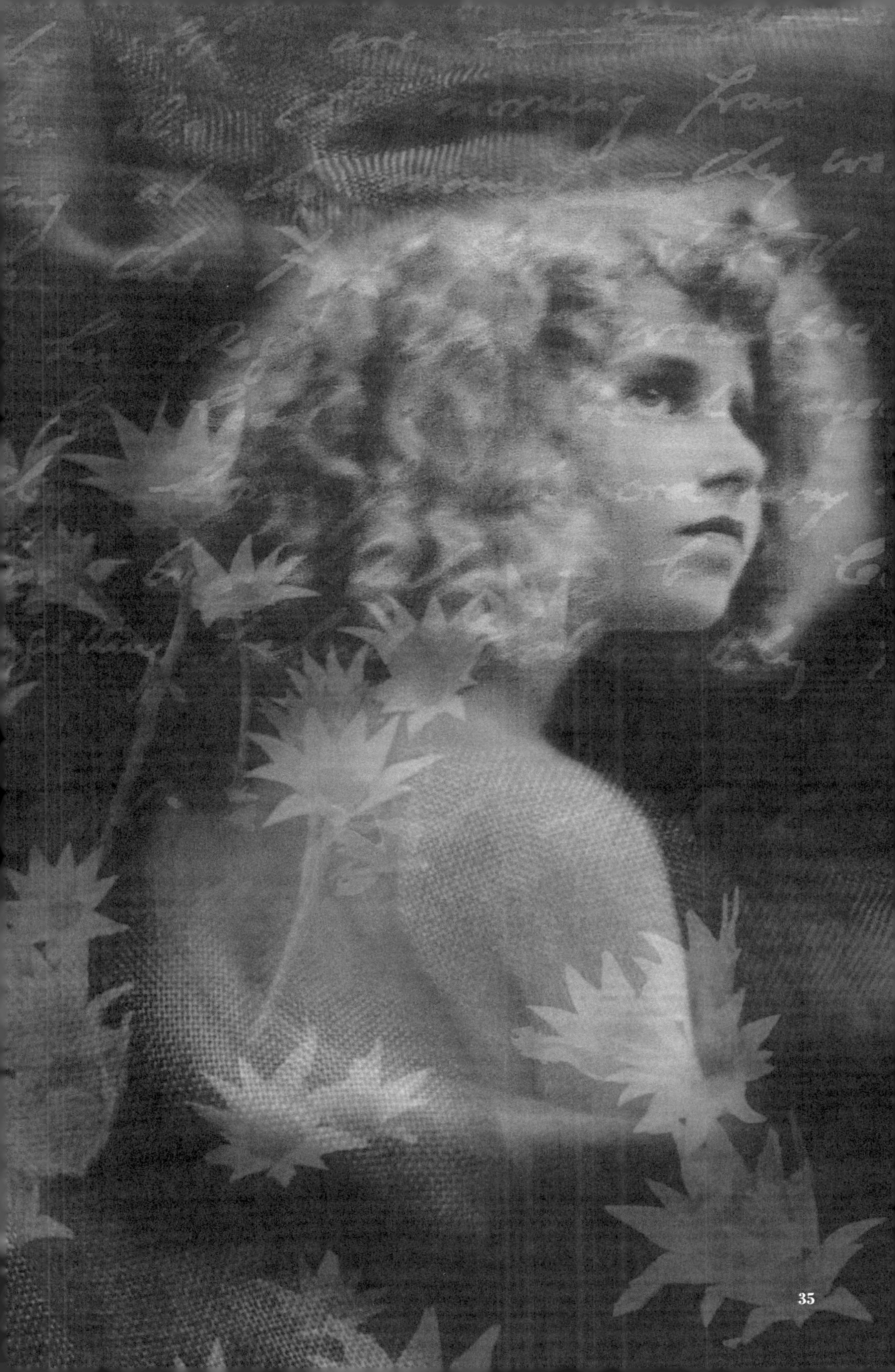

her mother's violin teaching materials
swamped the dining table
formed a surrogate tablecloth

scraps of sonatas and concertos
drift up to Muslin's bedroom
unbidden on Sunday mornings

*her mother reassigning the road they lived on
as the name of an ensemble*

half their youth spent playing at
local concerts, music festivals

weave of ambition, adrenalin

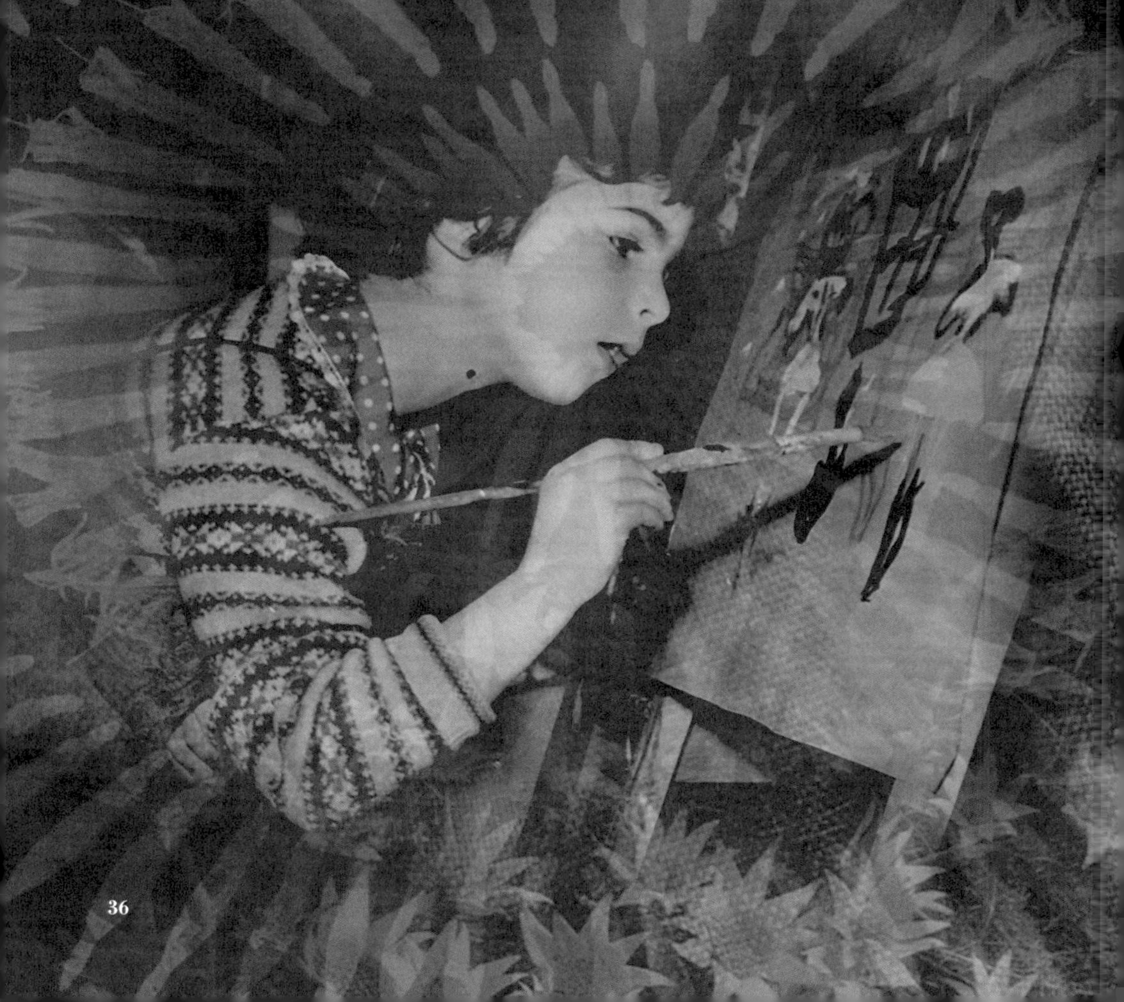

unending journeys to London to visit the grandparents
Muslin always felt sick in the car
her mother would pull her coffee flask out

                    (for the rest of her life
                    Muslin could not drink coffee
                    though she tried and tried)

                                        Australia never featured
                                        in her contracted world
                                        it was a no-place
                                        unfamiliar
                                        barely even exotic

                                        the people who lived there
                                        sounded cockney
                                        played crazily good tennis

now she has a bottlebrush
in her front garden
lorikeets gather there
green, blue, red, yellow

if you brush past the tree
they flap and fly away
squawking

Muslin's Lament

When I am dead will I still be mouthing poems? I discovered that they had a child who died. 'Remember me, remember me, but ah! forget my fate'.

Immersed in my performance I had a sudden memory lapse. My shame refused to lie down. 'How did you know how to write, who told you what to do?' Creativity was a formula, her mother thought, acquired through osmotic touch.

Jewishness hung heavily about her, a cumbersome overcoat. Sometimes an embrace felt more like suffocation. The fog of war curls round the fresh breath of thought.

My first published poem had a typo in it that decimated the flow. The art of performance thrilled but scared me: snakes twined round my legs. Meanwhile your grandfather shows his love for you by chasing you with an axe.

My aunt was bipolar and liaised between behavioural extremes. 'It's better to marry someone you dislike than not to marry', her mother said. Outrages flourished and fled: out-takes from a forgotten filming.

Your father fought in the German army, why hadn't I realised that? My mother's boyfriends wrote sentimental love poems from their billets. You furtively ate the salami, followed by a resounding slap.

The art of listening has never been more unfashionable. About your own culture you know too much (and yet too little). Each aunt, a silent heroine, hands down a legacy of hiding.

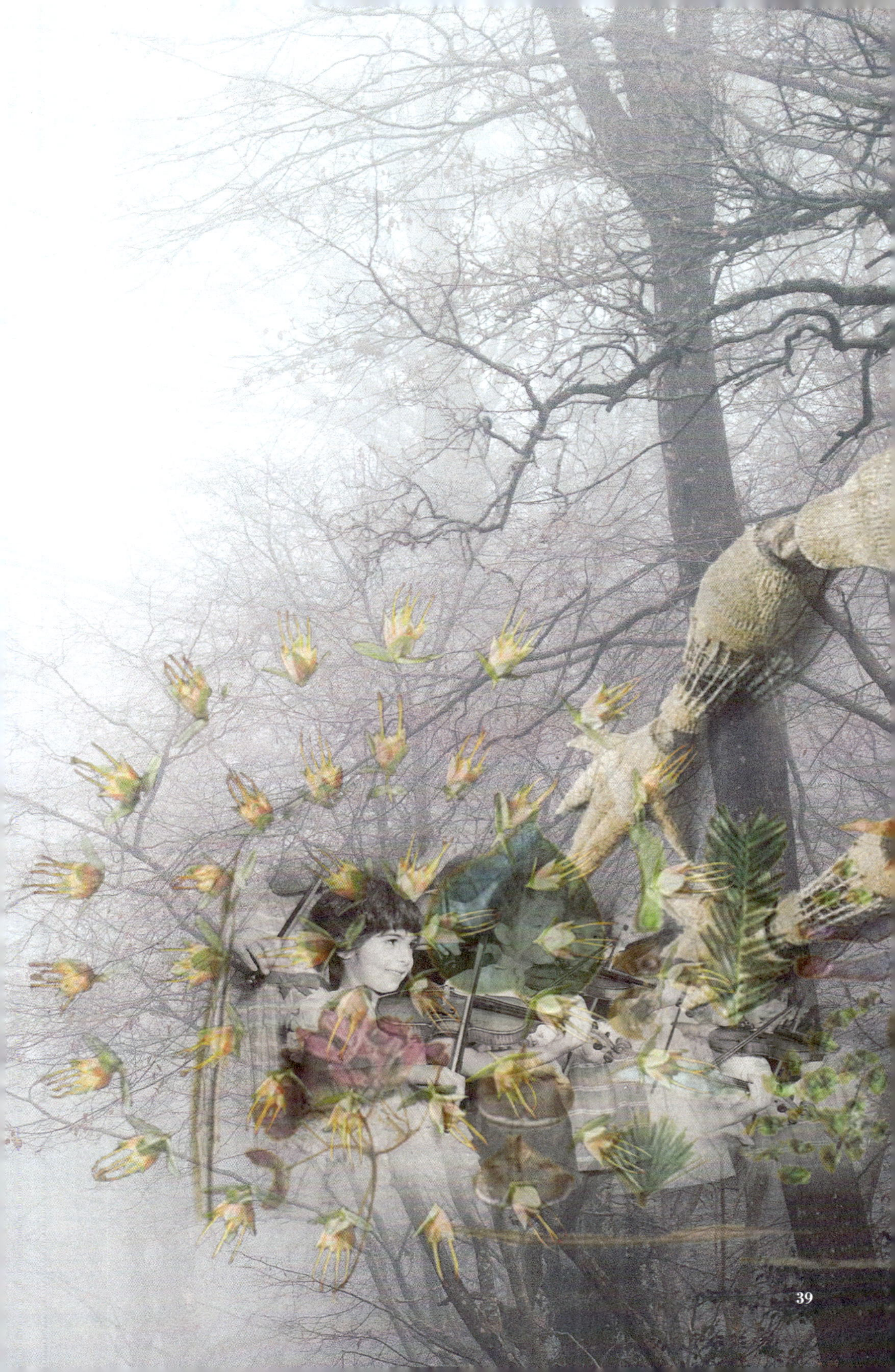

The Oriana

Bremen to Sydney, 1953. The Oriana. Teeming with ten-pound poms, hurrying to Australia to make their fortune.

She was a child of eight: what does Hessian remember?

ONE
Queen Elizabeth's coronation. Food, flags, beer, speeches. Dionysian celebration in an alien language.

Anxiety; strangeness; confusion.

TWO
The crossing of the Equator. People dressing up as surgeons, barbers, bears or judges jumping into the swimming pool. Grown-ups pouring buckets of water over her. A man in full costume as Neptune sitting ceremoniously on a throne with a forked weapon, holding court.

Bafflement; commotion; confusion.

THREE
Leaving the boat at Colombo and encountering black faces for the first time. Sheltering in a temple in a downpour. Silenced by the tight-lipped statues. Lunch in a spacious, cool room served by a man of colour dressed from head to toe in dazzling white.

Awe; curiosity; confusion.

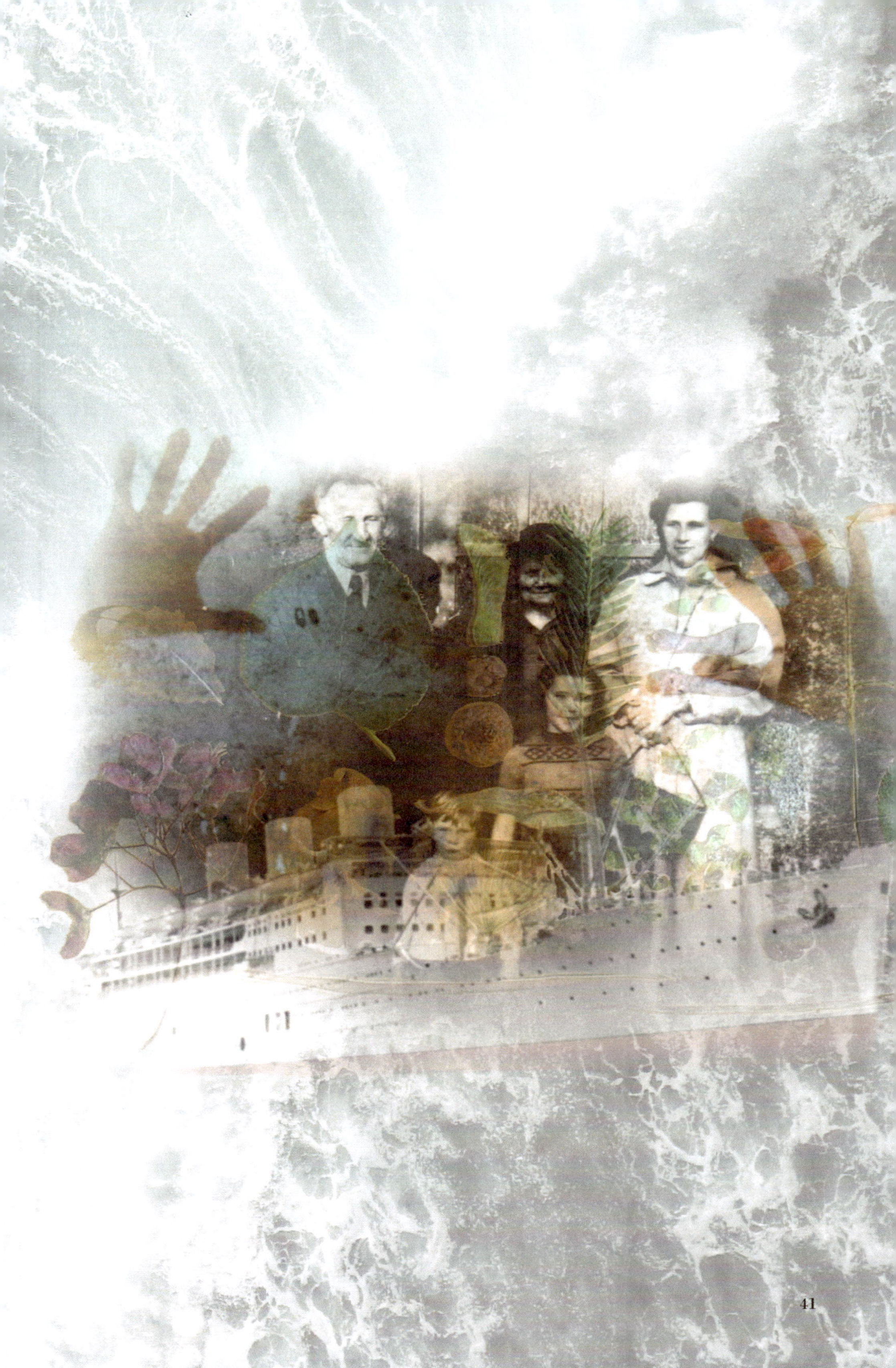

If

if we could re-shape the body
rethink its syntax and its grammar
conceive of it bottom to top
not top to bottom

if we could
dismantle it at will
parse each leg, each organ
expose those shy parts normally hidden

spread them thickly on a table
stumble on new joins
cheeky juxtapositions
until they become
other than ourselves

if we could raze
the boundaries of the nation
detonate its fetid hierarchies
erratic weathers

pull it apart as if it was a doll
honour each arm
each leg, each organ
then regroup them

that would be a revolution

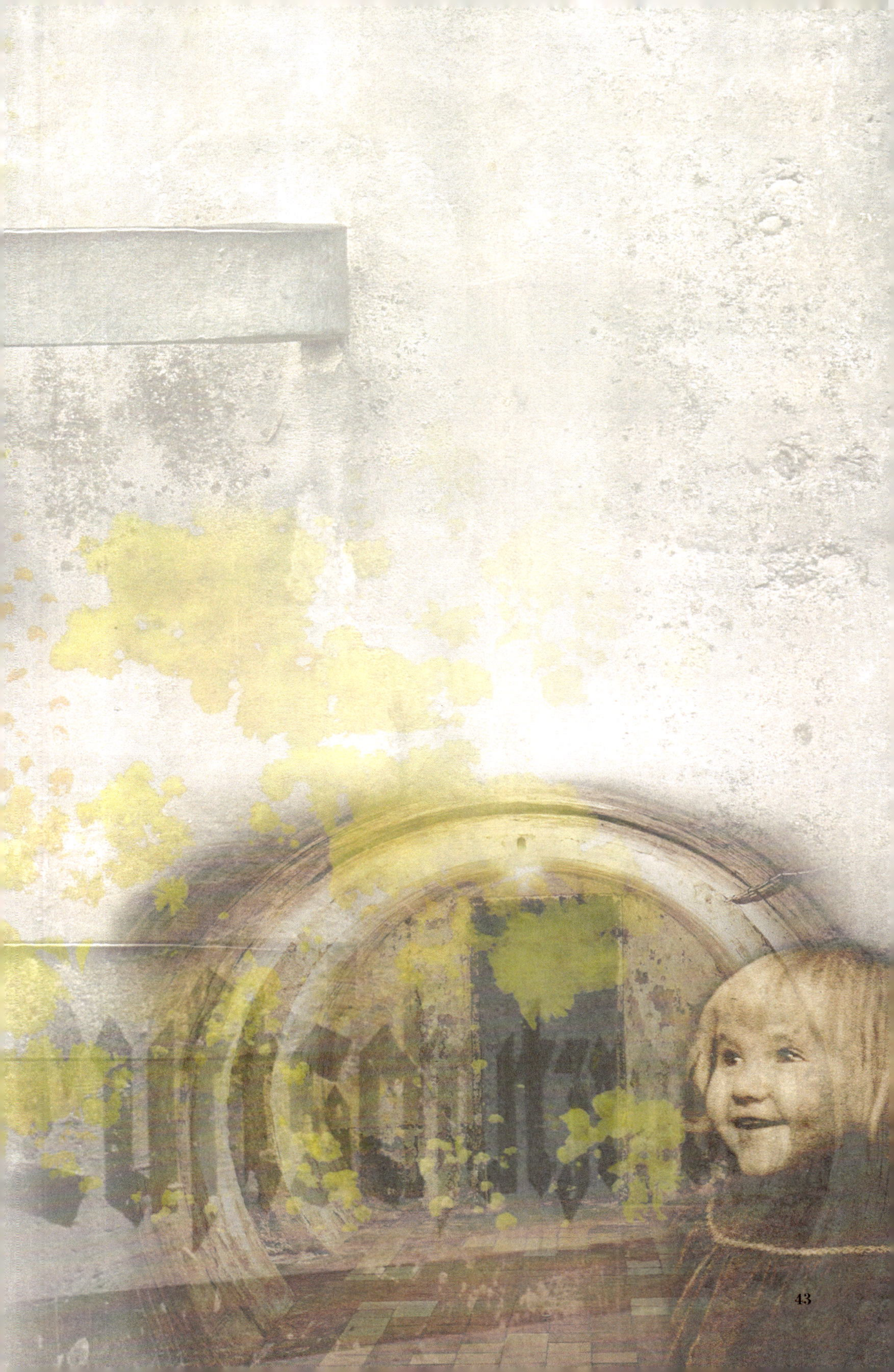

Walk to the End of Whistling

last night I walked to the end of whistling
fields menaced me on all sides
planted with severed thumbs

silence bent over into yoga positions
flashing its painted nails
steadying the wayward
winds of thought

on the horizon a homeless man
was collecting fingers
so that he could sew them into gestures
signalling rags of hope

time has never had much patience with me
everything was slo-mo or racing
I wondered if this was the gestation
of an idea or a rehearsal for
the end of the world

in the distance I saw a head
hoisted on a staff
swaying in the careless distance

sometimes it looked like yours
sometimes it mimicked mine

if your limbs could be pulled apart
from each other you said
they could be laid out
in tandem with my own

that's what it means to collaborate

a soldier ripped apart in an unnamed war
begged me to carry his
body parts home

last night I walked to the end of whistling
felder hobn mir fun ale zaytn gestrashet
mit abgetrennten daumen bepflanzt

silence bent over into yoga positions
blitzlendik mit di oysgefarbte negl
steadying the wayward
winde des denkens

on the horizon a homeless man
hot tsunoyfgezamlt finger
damit er sie in gesten nähen konnte
signalling rags of hope

time has never had much patience with me
alles war zeitlupe oder rasen
I wondered if this was the gestation
of an idea or a rehearsal for
dem sof fun der velt

in the distance I saw a head
hoisted on a staff
swaying in the careless distance

manchmal sah er aus wie deiner
teylmol hot es nokhgemakht mayns

if your limbs could be pulled apart
from each other you said
me ken zey tselaygn
im tandem mit meinen eigenen

ot dos iz der batayt fun mittsuarbetn

a soldier ripped apart in an unnamed war
begged me to carry his
body parts home

Gathering

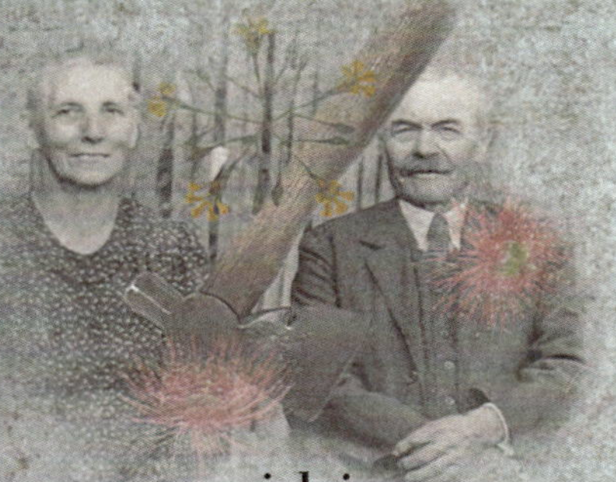

pasts and presents
hold hands
or put up fists
for a chilling fight

you pick images
as if they were needles
falling snow-like
in a digital garden

footage of the coiffured family
profiles at
carefully manicured angles

burn from the
stubborn
soil of family life

a photograph of a young violinist
bones you gathered in Tasmania
feathers from the wings of rainbow lorikeets

you try the images on
like torn, transparent overcoats
blur amplify the garments
underneath

strangers locked together
in transient monogamy
errant songfulness

determined to have their say
but not to gift us too much

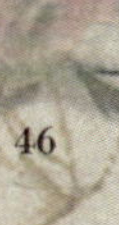

aunts and uncles
stare us down expectantly
from chaotic family albums

combat spreads
beyond the frame
that holds it

claiming a bond
we sometimes invite
sometimes repel

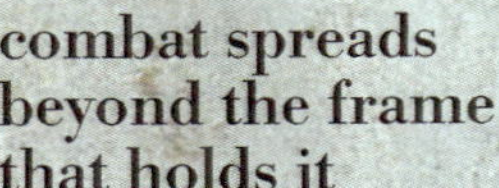

studied smiles mask
craggy marriages
queasy ruptures
mealy-mouthed collisions

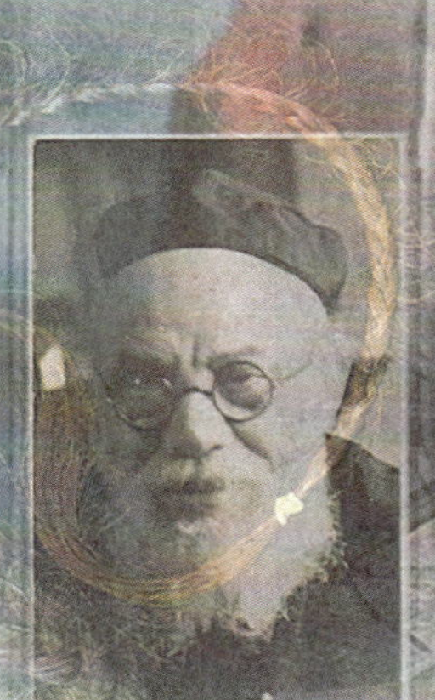

young faces reassert
swarms of former selves

the sealed secrets and desires
focus struggles to expose

character diffused in
the oozing stench
of context

*we look for what we
cannot find we
dig for what we
think we need to
know but what we
cannot apprehend
eludes us*

heat beyond fire
salt beyond seasoning

ABOUT THE ARTISTS

Sieglinde Karl-Spence spent her childhood years in her native Germany before emigrating to Australia with her family in 1953. She lives in Sydney.

Sieglinde trained as a jeweller, graduating in Jewellery and Silversmithing from Middlesex Polytechnic, London in 1978. Since the late 1980s her practice has focused on installation and performance, including works of a site-specific, transitory nature such as *Healing Mandala – 365 offerings*, Mildura Arts Festival, 1996 and *Red Bead Seed Offering*, Botanic Gardens, Darwin, 1997.

Sieglinde has exhibited extensively in Australia and internationally, including in the shows *Unfamiliar Territory*, 1992, Adelaide Biennial of Australian Art, Art Gallery of South Australia, and *Crossing Borders: History, Culture and Identity in Australian Contemporary Textile Art*, 1995, a major survey of Australian textiles that toured throughout the United States of America.

In 2002 Sieglinde was again part of the Adelaide Festival of the Arts, collaborating with chef Gay Bilson to produce the *Edible-lei Project* at the Queen Elizabeth Hospital, Adelaide. Sieglinde has taken part in many artist-in-residency projects in Tasmania, often working with the local community. Recently, Sieglinde has focused on making small transient mandala installations. Her work is represented in most of the major galleries in Australia including the National Gallery of Australia, Canberra; Art Gallery of Western Australia, Perth; Art Gallery of South Australia, Adelaide; Museum and Art Gallery of the Northern Territory, Darwin, NT; Queen Victoria Museum & Art Gallery, Launceston, Tasmania and Museum of Applied Arts & Sciences, Sydney, N.S.W.

Her website is at

http://sieglindekarl-spence.com.au

Hazel Smith is a poet, performer and new media artist. She has published five volumes of poetry including *The Erotics of Geography: poetry, performance texts, new media works*, Tinfish Press, Kaneohe, Hawaii, 2008 (with accompanying CD Rom), *Word Migrants*, Giramondo, 2016 and *Ecliptical*, ES-Press, Spineless Wonders, 2022. She has also published three CDs of poetry and performance work and numerous collaborative multimedia works, including *motions* and *novelling*, with Will Luers and Roger Dean, selected respectively in 2016 and 2022 for the Electronic Literature Collections 3 and 4. She is a member of austraLYSIS, the sound and multimedia arts group, has performed and presented her work extensively internationally, has been commissioned by the ABC to write several works for radio, and has been co-recipient of numerous Australia Council for the Arts grants.

In 1992 the ABC nominated her collaboration with Roger Dean, *Poet without Language*, for the prestigious Prix Italia award. In 2017, her multimedia collaboration with Will Luers and Roger Dean, *novelling*, was shortlisted for the Turn on Literature Prize, an initiative of the Creative Europe Program of the European Union. In 2018 *novelling* was awarded First Prize in the Electronic Literature Organisation's Robert Coover Award. In 2023 her collaboration with Will Luers and Roger Dean, *Dolphins in the Reservoir*, was shortlisted for the UK New Media Writing Prize.

From 2007 to 2017 Hazel was a Research Professor in the Writing and Society Research Centre at Western Sydney University where she is now an Emeritus Professor. She is the author of several academic and pedagogical books including *Hyperscapes in the Poetry of Frank O'Hara: difference, homosexuality, topography*, Liverpool University Press, 2000, *The Writing Experiment: strategies for innovative creative writing*, Allen and Unwin, 2005 and *The Contemporary Literature-Music Relationship: intermedia, voice, technology, cross-cultural exchange*, Routledge, 2016. With Roger Dean she co-authored *Improvisation, Hypermedia and the Arts since 1945*, Routledge, 1997 and co-edited *Practice-led Research, Research-led Practice in the Creative Arts*, Edinburgh University Press, 2009.

She is a co-editor of the creative arts journal of online sound, text and image, *soundsRite*, based at Western Sydney University. Hazel previously pursued a career as a professional violinist.

Her website is at

http://www.australysis.com

NOTES AND REFERENCES

The eleven sections of *Heimlich Unheimlich* move between the stories of Muslin or Hessian though sometimes the stories are intertwined. A work of poetry, fiction and visual images with an autobiographical overhang, *Heimlich Unheimlich* draws on photographs, letters and other material from Hazel and Sieglinde's family archives.

Preface

Includes photographic material from the family albums of Sieglinde Karl-Spence and Hazel Smith.

Sigmund Freud, 'The "Uncanny"', 1919. Available at https://web.mit.edu/allanmc/www/freud1.pdf, pp.1-21.

Marianne Hirsch, *Family Frames: Photography, Narrative and Postmemory*, Cambridge, Mass. and London: Harvard University Press, 2002. Hirsch says, 'In my reading, post-memory is distinguished from memory by generational distance and from history by deep personal connection…Postmemory characterizes the experience of those who grow up dominated by narratives that preceded their birth, whose own belated stories are evacuated by the stories of the previous generation shaped by traumatic events that can be neither understood nor recreated', p. 22.

Sieglinde Karl-Spence, Hazel Smith, Roger Dean and austraLYSIS. *Heimlich Unheimlich*, video, https://www.australysis.com/hear-see-read/aLYS-works/worksNewM.html, 2019. Original conception devised by Sieglinde Karl-Spence (image) and Hazel Smith (text) with digital editing by Claire Grocott. Image montage and processing by Roger Dean; composed and improvised sound by Roger Dean and austraLYSIS. The performers are Hazel Smith (text), Sandy Evans (saxophone), Phil Slater (trumpet) and Greg White (computers). The sound is from an austraLYSIS performance at the MARCS Institute for Brain, Behaviour and Development, Western Sydney University, 2019. The video also includes some text not included in this volume, such as the following passage:

Muslin felt a profound ambivalence about her Jewishness, and that division became a home. It repelled her but also invited her in like the most intrusive sunlight. Her position was always slightly off-balance, as if she was standing on one leg. She was an atheist and committed to the athleticism of free thought. But Jewishness was a burden and bequest that she must dig her way towards. She owed it something, felt an obscure loyalty towards it, but did not want it to inter her.

Archive of the Evergreen

Includes photographic material from the family album of Hazel Smith.

Heimlich Unheimlich

Includes photographic material from the family album of Sieglinde Karl-Spence.

This collage, like several of the other collages, includes a mandala constructed by Sieglinde Karl-Spence from natural materials.

The handwriting is a page from Hazel Smith's *Tapa Notebook* in the Special Collections, New Zealand Electronic Poetry Centre records, University of Auckland, 2014.

The poem alludes to Freud's essay 'The "Uncanny"', https://web.mit.edu/allanmc/www/freud1.pdf, which explores the relationship between the terms heimlich and unheimlich. It also quotes from the essay: 'we call it unheimlich, you call it heimlich' and 'the name for everything that ought to have remained hidden and secret', p.3.

From Rubble to Reliving

The collage, which evokes post-war Germany, includes photographic material mainly from the family albums of Sieglinde Karl-Spence but also from that of Hazel Smith.

It contains a handwritten page from Hazel Smith's *Tapa Notebook* in the Special Collections, New Zealand Electronic Poetry Centre records, University of Auckland, 2014.

Like several of the other collages, this one includes photography of constructed body parts created by Sieglinde Karl-Spence. Some of these body parts, made from hessian and muslin, were originally created for the *Heimlich Unheimlich* exhibition.

In the collage on the second page, the inscription is taken from a German children's book published in 1925. Sieglinde translates 'Kindheit' as 'Childhood' and 'Des Kindes Kleine und grosse Welt – seine Luft und sein Leid' as 'The child's small and large world – its air and its burden'.

The text uses information from the article by Max Chalmers, 'What Happens when you leave Nazi Quotes on Tabloid News Stories? The Readers Love it', *new.matilda.com*, August 12th 2015.

The White Rose

The collage includes photographic material from the family album of Sieglinde Karl-Spence.

'a raid on the inarticulate' is from T.S. Eliot, 'East Coker', *Collected Poems 1909-1962*, London: Faber and Faber, 1963, p.203.

The White Rose resistance movement, formed by Hans Scholl in 1942, consisted mainly of students. They spoke out, and distributed leaflets, against the policies of the Nazis. White Rose members included Sophie Scholl, Hans Scholl, Kurt Huber, Christoph Probst, Willi Graf, and Alexander Schmorell. Hans Scholl, Sophie Scholl and Christoph Probst were all executed.

The Vengeful, Directive Angel

Includes photographic material from the family album of Hazel Smith. This photograph was included in the 2nd edition of Eta Cohen's *The First-Year Violin Method* published by W. Paxton and Co. in London in the 1950s (the first edition was published in 1941). Eta Cohen (1916-2012) was Hazel Smith's mother.

The poem uses information from an article by Richard A. Serrano, '"Sweet Lady" Hid Nazi Past', *Los Angeles Times*, September 20th, 2006, https://www.latimes.com/archives/la-xpm-2006-sep-20-me-nazi20-story.html.

Mill of Memory

Includes photographic material and letters from the family album of Hazel Smith.

The photograph of Leeds city centre, 'Boar Lane, looking east, 1951', is reproduced by kind permission of Leeds Libraries, UK, www.leodis.net.

The Lone Ranger was an American Western television series very popular in the UK in the 1950s.

'The wind of change is blowing through this continent' is a quotation from Harold Macmillan's speech to the South African parliament, February 3rd, 1960, https://web-archives.univ-pau.fr/english/TD2doc1.pdf.

Walk to the End of Whistling

Includes photographic material from the family albums of Sieglinde Karl-Spence and Hazel Smith.

In the right-hand column, the poem in English in the lefthand column is rendered in a mixture of English, German and Yiddish. We are grateful to Myra Woolfson for her assistance with the translation from English into Yiddish, and Inge Stocker for her assistance with the translation from English into German.

Muslin's Lament

Includes photographic material from the family album of Hazel Smith.

'Remember me, remember me, but ah! forget my fate' is a quotation from the aria, 'When I am laid in earth', known as Dido's Lament, from Henry Purcell's opera, *Dido and Aeneas*, libretto Nahum Tate, circa 1688.

The Oriana

Includes photographic material from the family album of Sieglinde Karl-Spence.

If

Includes photographic material from the family album of Sieglinde Karl-Spence.

Gathering

Includes photographic material from the family albums of Sieglinde Karl-Spence and Hazel Smith.

* 9 7 8 0 6 4 8 8 0 7 9 9 5 *